THROW THIS BOOK IN THE TRASH

TORREY LEE

First published in 2022 by Iffy Books

Copyright © 2022 by Torrey Lee

ISBN 979-8-218-25262-5

Edited and typeset by Wrate's Editing Services, London

www.wrateseditingservices.co.uk

This book is dedicated to the world, and is a direct result of the world. I sincerely thank the Gods/God for allowing me to be an instrument of service. To the readers, thank you and enjoy.

"The greatest lie told to the inhabitants of the world is that certain chaos will happen if each person exists on their own terms."

Torrey Lee

EDITOR'S NOTE
BY DANIELLE WRATE

Not many authors would encourage their readers to throw their book in the trash, but then again Torrey Lee is no ordinary author. His short philosophical treatise came to him one Saturday morning in a kind of mystical download. But if you're looking for a guru or someone to tell you what to do or how to think then this is not the book for you. In fact, Torrey's creation is the antithesis of the myriad self-help books that saturate the market. Although Torrey reflects on major themes such as faith and religion, love and sex, and fear and courage, it is not his intention to tell you how to live your life. Instead, Torrey encourages you to ignore everybody and everything — even him — so that you can tune into your own voice and start living authentically on your own terms. Torrey has shared his wisdom, but ingeniously, only so that you may reject it and go in search of your own . . .

FOREWORD

BY OLIVER BIRD

Self-help is a modern and expanding method of categorizing books. But do most of the books that fall into this category genuinely belong in it? In Western societies today, we often think we want someone to tell us the best way to live our lives. Each year, we buy millions of dollars' worth of paperbacks, hardbacks, and e-books, in the hope that the answer or answers to our perceived or real problems have already been written and published. However, when people we know give us advice personally, do we take it? It often seems easier to follow generalized advice loosely and go along with the crowd, but is this really *self*-help?

I first met Torrey Lee in a busy street at night in Brazil, where I live. It was a Saturday and I'd not long arrived in the neighborhood and bought a drink. The place in question is an area where people gather and mostly stay outside in very informal settings. I hadn't been out long and had been expecting a relaxed evening of laughter and music with a friend of mine, to distract myself from the usual stresses of the working week. "Excuse me, y'all speak English?" was Torrey's introduction. Almost immediately, he started talking to me about history, philosophy, and the world, and he has hardly stopped since. We had deep conversations for most of the night and have been good friends and debating partners from that moment.

The book you are about to read is the result of the culmination of the colorful life experiences, studies, and actions of this forthright yet observant character. Yet for me, a great book, orator, or even film does not necessarily need to draw on years of specific experience. Even if one did, everyone's experiences have their own colors, tones, and complexities, so there's no guarantee they can be directly relevant to the reader, listener, or viewer. In this case, as a matter of fact, this is Torrey's first book, but far from the first time he has discussed the topics within it. His insights are at times intriguing, refreshing, or shocking. What I personally find important is the ability to provoke thoughts and reflection, which this book, along with the author, achieves admirably.

INTRODUCTION

Thank you for getting this book. I experience joy, confirmation of my existence, and strength when I connect with people. I am not a specialist, expert, or professor in any of the topics covered in this book. This book was written because I woke up one morning and it was in my head. I had not been trying to come up with any ideas to write this book. I am actually working on a novel, which will probably be harder to write, because this book was unknowingly impregnated into my consciousness.

I play my part in sharing this knowledge and wisdom, but most of this book is outside of me. I am not at all concerned about the philosophical idea behind my last statement or any of the statements in this book. I believe this book was written not to educate, but to inspire you to become aware of yourself, focus on yourself, and never relinquish that focus for anyone or anything. This may not yet make sense to you, but this is an accurate expression of what is inside me at this exact moment. Read this book carefully. Be very slow and cautious to believe or agree with what you read.

When I woke up one Saturday morning, this text had been given to me, probably because of where I was in my life at that moment. I would type this manuscript as the words appeared to me, regardless of any backlash I feared or struggle I felt with completing this work.

I long to see a world of pure creation. We exist in a world of Johnny-come-latelies. We are focused on the next big thing. People tend to categorize other people by famous individuals. Like, who is the next Bill Gates? Or, hey, is he the next Mark Zuckerberg? That is so—excuse my language but obscenities provide vivid expressions—fucking disgusting. There is only one Mark Z and there is only one Bill Gates. There will never be any other people like them. Thank goodness, as the whole science of cloning could have been created for that very purpose, instead of for technology and medical advances. The very thought of waking up to be someone else . . . why would I want to be anyone other than exactly who I am? You would have to take all the things about that person; pleasant, unpleasant, known, and unknown. Also, take into consideration that you still exist as well, so your existence is still present. By wanting to be someone else your existence is established, and being someone else doesn't destroy it. If it did you would cease. Then the other person would be just that, another person, not you. Take a second and think about that.

I imagine something Divine screaming at everyone on this Earth and saying, "Stop just doing things, stop trying to fit the mold, stop trying not to fit the mold. Who cares about accolades and degrees? Who cares if you have millions of followers on your social media account? Be, create, and express."

Instead, people say, "I do this because this book says it's right." "I do that because a preacher/priest, motivational speaker, or professor said so." "I do this because everybody else is doing it." "I do this because I am terrified of pain, misfortune, death, and embarrassment." People are living their lives based on what is easy to convey at a social gathering. I urge you instead to listen to that voice inside of you.

Consider an example: When was the last time you heard a person say, "I am not concerned about investing too much for retirement; I will be fine."? Everyone would ridicule that person as a loser, broke, or dumb, and yet some people invest their whole life only to end up with nothing. They either gamble it away or give it to some organization to do God-knows-what with. It can be difficult to create your own values, likes, goals, language, dislikes, and ideas. You might have to ignore everybody and everything.

There is no format to this book. There is no structure to this book. There is no book. You can't prove me wrong unless I agree to become part of your belief system. And I don't. I have my own system. Maybe you should be too . . . instead of following everything and everyone else. For all you smart asses, that includes following me as well.

CHAPTER 1
FAITH & RELIGION

"Faith and religion both are built on love, peace, and community, but both have ignited more killings, wars, and divisions than just about anything else in the world. . . damn!!!" Torrey Lee

I might as well start with the topic of faith and religion and get it out of the way. I don't think anything is wrong with faith or religion. People link themselves or associate themselves with faith and religion in many ways. They go together, but that's another book.

I began this chapter by jotting down ideas on paper and realized that I just had to start typing. The act of jotting down ideas was my fear. As I stated in the introduction, this book was given to me. All I had to do was type it. Thinking about it would be me trying to make something up. And why would I do that? Like I said, I would only do this because of fear, shame, disbelief, or possibly blindness (i.e., not being able to see all of the story!). This could be my fear of saying the wrong thing, insulting people, or making God/the Gods mad at me. You know, the usual things we tell ourselves when it comes to faith and religion.

Yes, faith and religion are difficult topics. There are so many variations—some for the same God and some for different ones. People are ready to kill and ostracize you for being on what they believe is the wrong side, having different ideas, or different feelings toward what they believe. Outside of all the madness, something magical exists. Faith—that is, to believe in something not readily present—is beautiful. Especially today. We believe ourselves to function on science, but really everything we do is faith. Even science tells us that nothing is 100 percent certain. The possibility always exists for something to go in the opposite direction of what was thought, planned, or proved.

So, why believe in God/the Gods? Many people would agree that something deep down produces feelings of something higher than the Universe, human life, or alien life forms. We use science and reason to explain and justify just about everything in life. Religion can also be a justification for what is supernatural. Hence, what causes so much discord. We tell others that their religion is false or that their interpretation of their religion is inaccurate. The mystic wonders in life all seem to fade, but the idea of God/the Gods doesn't. Many people prefer to access

God/the Gods through a set of rules and customs. In my opinion, I tend to think of religions as nothing more than social clubs. If you study the foundations of most religions, you will see they were more like social clubs than anything else. My point is not to argue whether God/the Gods exists, or which is real. My point is to make you think about what you think and feel. If we spent more time trying to understand each other's form of faith/nonfaith or religion/irreligion, then maybe we would gain more insight into God/the Gods. Possibly we would see more clearly, or at least stop tearing each other down over these concepts.

As a young man, I went to church because my mother made me go. I had fun playing with the other kids, but all I could remember was that I should try to be a good boy as opposed to a bad one. This involved doing the regular things that constitute being a good boy—not lying, swearing, stealing, or doing anything your parents told you not to do. I think that is where most kids start with religion. The funny thing is that I think I should've stayed right there. Even the King James Bible states, "Verily I say unto you, except ye be converted, and become as little children, ye shall not enter into the kingdom of heaven" (Matthew 18:3).

Kids just want to love, play, laugh, and not feel pain all day long. When I grew older, my mind naturally directed deeper conversations about God/the Gods in life. This continued into my troubled teen years. I felt as if I had been cursed with some evil spiritual journey, with some Divine purpose or a heightened sense of wisdom to be discovered. I also felt like it was a forced journey. After about three years of college, I enrolled in a seminary college and made really good grades. I loved helping people by words of encouragement and visiting people in the hospital. I was struggling, however, with depression. I would lay on my couch after studying for upwards of 6 to 12 hours, contemplating life and faith. I went to speak to the dean of the seminary, and his advice was that men of God had to have their hearts broken by God. At the time, I thought that was a crock of shit. As I look back, I honestly just did not want to give my life to God/the Gods in that manner. I didn't care for religious piety. I was 25 and I wanted more life experiences.

I denounced Christianity. I was doing what I had been doing since I had been given the choice to choose. I just could not swallow the fact that God wanted me to love him/her or I would go to hell. That seemed like force to me, and if God/the Gods was so powerful, it/they would want people to want to love and serve. It would not want people to have faith so that they could get a pass into heaven and avoid hell given we really don't have a solid clue of either. I follow the teachings of Christ today because I want to and because the love and faith I have now have grown organically. I naturally found my way to a relationship with God through Christ. I did not experience a tragedy and suddenly run to God. I also did not start to fear my sins and think I would end up in hell. Just like meeting a woman, I started having internal conversations, and over a period of time, my relationship with God developed. It did not happen overnight, and it did not blossom into love overnight. It's a relationship for me, and with time, work, love, and faith, it gets better. I have bad days, bad months, and bad years, just like with any great relationship. However, the love and joy I feel keeps me connected.

Now, how does that align with all of the craziness in the world? It doesn't! This is my personal sacred relationship. Just as I wouldn't share my wife with another man, my relationship with God/Christ is not for the world. I think it is silly and prideful for people to do that anyway. Would I share Christ? Heck, yes. A relationship with him is yours if you want it. However, I refuse to force him on people, condemn people, or tear people down in his name. God/Christ exists, and I am comfortable with them judging and ruling. So, if you are a Muslim, Hindu, Buddhist, Jew, atheist, or whatever, I have love for you. Period!

If you are waiting for me to advise or presume I am a guru, stop waiting. Most people have already read enough of these types of books to become a guru themselves. What do you think you should do? Are you okay? Are you sure that deep down your voice isn't already telling you something different than what you are doing? If not, fine. But if so, then what should you do about it?

I will end this chapter with this. You may seek help to get inside yourself, but ultimately, I think you have to be the one to produce what you need. How can my life map for my specific path help get you to your specific place? You're the only one inside of you, and you are the only one who can get inside. So, you truly are the only one who can say whether something is true within you. Not a book, a religion, an expert, friends, or family. Nothing and nobody. It's just you. The previous statements are not indications of self-help. Logically speaking, self-help is a false idea and doesn't exist! I would rather you call this book a piece of shit or wipe your ass with it before you label it a self-help book.

CHAPTER 2
LOVE & SEX

"You just can't sell a product, book, movie, or music anymore without talking about or using sex . . ."
Torrey Lee

D o we all need love and sex? Or just one of them? What really is love or sex? No one definition of love or sex seems to be universal. Can you touch love? Sex is just as mysterious. The whole thing: role-playing, using objects, multiple partners, same-sex sex, underage sex, orgy sex, ritual sex, pain sex, and so on. Is sex nothing more than a physical high or experience? There are so many reasons for sex and the kinds of sex in which people engage that we cannot have a one-size-fits-all definition. This same thing applies to love. The books we read, the television shows we watch, and the experiences of others are just that—experiences.

What does this mean for an individual? Well, let's

start with love. It has been said that you know when you have love and you know when you don't. Is that based on our emotions, what our eyes tell us, or what our minds conclude? I think it's all of that, and more. I believe that love is complicated only when people try to figure it out, as opposed to experiencing it. Babies know what love is. Not because of food, but because they just know. You can see a baby gravitate toward one parent more than the other. Now, a baby's mind isn't as developed as an adult's mind. When I say "mind," I mean it all. So, what does a toddler feel when a stranger gives them candy? Does that suddenly mean that mommy and daddy aren't the loves of their life? I once dated a woman whom I held all night. I didn't even know this until she told me. She said that whenever she moved, I would come after her until she was in my arms again. At that time in my life, I disliked cuddling for long periods of time. Explanation? Possibly love.

Sex is the same. We all pretty much have the same tools or capabilities, with some variations. So how do we have the best sex? How can we find the best sex partner? Where do our sexual desires come from? Deep down, something is unique about all of us. With technology in our faces, with television, computers, smartphones, tablets, and now smartwatches, we tend to adapt to what we see and hear regularly. We adapt to whatever is around us. Maybe we are or are not the sexual beings we portray ourselves to be. Have you ever had a relationship in which the sex was one thing, but later your partner said, "I did this just for you"? It's as simple (or even as complicated) as we have made our lives. I think sex is what you like when you like it. To me love is what it means to me when I feel it. I don't maintain the/a idea of love. I allow myself to exist, experience, enjoy, dislike, and feel it. You can always keep doing what you have always done. You define what love is and what sex means to you. I am always looking for someone who shares the same definition or who at least is willing to learn. I make sure I am looking inward and truly believe and know what my own heart and desires are first. Because if I don't, then existing through others' ideas is all I will ever do.

Bonus: This does not mean you can sexually assault someone because that's what you like or that you can play with people's hearts/minds because you want to.

If other people are not conscious of your desires, your heart, or your intentions, then you are still living in fear and enslavement. If you truly are free, you believe there is someone for you to love. You know that you can really be loved for who you are. You will not have to act, do this or do that, become this, or obtain this or that. You can just be, and someone will just be with you.

I refuse to tell you how to go about this. And any damn way, I don't know how to! I am willing to bet my life that the right way is inside you. This is something else to make you think. We are superior to animals, right? Dogs love and yet they don't read, have money, take male enhancement pills, work out, have degrees, own fast cars, get lipo, hold huge bank accounts, post hundreds of pictures on social media, and have access to all the accessories and resources that we do. Again, maybe you may need these things, who am I to say shooting chemicals in your ass is wrong??

CHAPTER 3
FAMILY & FRIENDS

"We're family, so I should be able to treat you any way I want and you stay in the relationship, right?"
Torrey Lee

The old saying goes, "I wouldn't have enemies if it weren't for my friends." The Judeo-Christian bible even states that "a man's foes shall be they of his own household" (Matthew 10:36NKJV). The truth is that we spend our adult lives trying to either duplicate our childhood or run far away from it. Yet we still go to great lengths for our friends and family. A young lady I once knew told her mother that her grandfather was molesting her. She said that her brother later sold her sexually when she got older. I guess he thought she was already screwed over, so why not profit from her? Excuse me, people, but I have to say, "Sick fucks!" This goes for her mom, grandfather, and her brother. This had happened by the time she was 16. I was puzzled and first wondered whether this could be true. My left brain told me that even if it wasn't true, her mind was sick. Some things you just don't lie about. Something like this could happen to you in some shape, form, or fashion. I wasn't rich and she never asked me for money. So, if she was playing me, what for? As I recall, the information slipped out one day while we were having lunch. She said she didn't want sympathy and didn't want to discuss it too deeply. She went on to say that she told her mom, and her mom's reply was, "He is almost dead anyway; just don't worry about it." Now the kicker is this: She still has a relationship with her mom and her brother. You would think these atrocities must never have happened. I am sure many people are living with terrible wrongs at the expense of friends and family. But shit, man!!!

So, now another view. The holidays are advertised as the best times to be with friends and family, and I don't doubt that for some or most of you, they are. But what about the ones for whom they aren't? You cannot pick your biological family, and I don't think we really pick our friends. Sorry, social media, we don't. I think everyone knows this deep down, but for personal reasons, we often continue to maintain bad and hurtful relationships. Some people read books, go to therapy, pray, and do everything they can think of, to no avail. So why do we continue to stay in hard relationships? Why do we stay connected to family members who have hurt us more than made us feel good? I am talking about serious pain and not the silly stuff. DNA will never be an excuse for me to stay in a hurtful relationship. Being family isn't an excuse to live in hell and pain.

As beautiful and bright as that young lady was, she was just plain afraid or too mentally damaged possibly. She definitely understood good and loving friendships and family relationships. She didn't like what happened to her, but out of that experience, we can conclude that she now knows what she wants from relationships. To feel valued, safe, and not violated, and to be loved and cared for. One can guess that her mom and brother haven't changed that much. Even so, how does a person truly recover from allowing their child to be molested by their father? From selling their sister for money? I am quite sure religious people are chiming in here, saying that forgiveness and restoration of relationships through God/the Gods is possible. Maybe through a miracle, but most likely, hell no! In this young lady's case, what relationship is there to restore? Restore means to get back to a good relationship. Meaning that a good relationship would have had to exist in the first place. What if we demanded, not from others, but from ourselves, to have the best people in our life at all cost? What if we were willing to go around the world and back to have love, understanding, commonality, and everything else we need as individuals from our relationships? I mean, if the city, state, country, and continent didn't produce rewarding family ties and friendships, then would you be willing to go to greater lengths to find them?

For me relationships are a two-way street, directly and indirectly. No matter my strengths or weaknesses, relationships must be beneficial and rewarding to both parties. As a result, I have been blessed to have family added to my life that don't share my DNA. However, they share in love with me through all seasons. Yes, I had to leave my country, continent, and comfort zone to discover these people. This has made my life so sweet. I have new brothers, sisters, aunts, and cousins. These people strive for relations of harmony and love through all seasons. I am not judged, ridiculed, or disrespected. We just love each other and choose compassion as our mode of interaction. Are there tough times and disagreements? Hell, yeah! Nothing is without problems, but the relationships are primarily of love and compassion. Not disfunction and discord. Thank you, Jesus, for all of them!!!

I will leave you with this: How is your life influenced by your family and friends? If you were in relationships that were totally fulfilling for your family, friends, and yourself, what would your life be like? How far would you go to have fulfilling relationships in your life?

This didn't naturally come out of me. If you feel like the value of your friendships and family isn't that important, then this is fine too. If you really believe you don't need family and friends, then trust me, it is your life. People definitely live far away from everyone else, and who are we to tell them they need people in their lives? You know, I cannot tell you what you need to do, and neither can anyone else. Then again, maybe they can and that's what you need, for someone to tell you what your life should be.

CHAPTER 4
PASSION & WORK

"If more people really loved their jobs, what they did at work, and the products or services that were produced as a result, then just maybe . . .?" Torrey Lee

H it the damn snooze button, thinks the mind of the modern work slave. We laugh here, maybe. But what is really funny is that some people I know do consider themselves to be slaves to their jobs. This isn't some big revelation.

I once dated a woman who was an overachiever, so to speak. She was the person already working in corporate America in college, while others were interning. She had naturally worked hard her entire life. Her parents never imposed this lifestyle on her. She studied harder than her peers, placed herself in all kinds of organizations as a high school and college student, read books like most people watch television and listen to music, and trained her brain and body for what she thought was success. People around us wondered, besides my good looks and charming personality, why she was with me. While we were dating, however, I paid close attention to her behind the scenes. Sometimes she seemed overly silent. At times, I felt like we were in a graveyard. She was overly awkward sometimes, too, as if she wasn't comfortable in her skin. She worked in the insurance industry while simultaneously earning an MBA degree. During our second year of dating, I built a restaurant with a friend. What was interesting to me is that my venture captured her interest and inspired her to start a business as well. One day, while I was out of town, I called her to say hello and noticed that she sounded down. I asked her what was wrong, and she said she wished I would hurry up and marry her so that she would not have to keep herself busy with her business and stuff. Wow! All of that energy and time she gave to her work and business and it seemed to be something just to keep her busy. It made sense to me. Ms. Perfect was miserable but had never been honest with herself. This explained why she hit the snooze button every morning. I could never match her desire and sacrifice my life for what books and mentors said was the blueprint to success. This was true regardless of how unstable I may have appeared to be at that time. As much as she liked achieving, learning, and working at a high-caliber job, she was not happy or fulfilled. How could I marry her? I didn't, by the way.

I definitely think that at some point, we all need

jobs, but I have always believed that jobs are temporary. They are more so for adolescent youths who are training to be adults. Or for the elderly who are working to socialize. And, no, they shouldn't have to work to get medicine, bill money, or any other necessity to survive. Imagine—unless cleaning toilets is your heaven/oasis—deriving any happiness or peace from cleaning up shit. People have a greater purpose than cleaning up shit after other people. Whether you're working as a delivery driver or as a chief operating officer of a corporation, I think you are wasting your time if you cannot make a living doing what you love and what you feel passionate about. We raise our children to attend college and earn a degree as a doctor or a lawyer, mainly because of money, security, and honour. In my opinion, of which means absolutely nothing unless passion and love are involved. And feeling happy to clean the shit from toilets because you can provide for your family isn't an excuse, either. Animals provide for their offspring. Do we really want to be compared to animals in that regard? Animals don't have an alarm clock or have to clean the shit out of restrooms to do it, either. The suffering and feelings of discomfort that can accompany a person finding and living out their passion are worth it, and many times more. The passion inside of you is priceless! Or again, maybe it's not. We are all waiting for you to share this passion with the rest of the world. The following is a formula I have used.

Disclaimer: This is not advice!!

I gave myself a hypothetical 100 million dollars and asked what I would do. I continued to ask myself this question over the course of several years and noticed that my answer didn't change—even with a ton of money. I also hypothetically divested myself of everything—to leave myself nothing—and yes, you are right, it brought me to the same conclusions. That was my way of looking inside myself. No book or person gave me that. I think most books get people to this point, and some are filled with complex ideas about how to find your passion.

How can I tell you what makes you feel good? What you dream or fantasize about all the time? Some people have to go to great lengths to find this in themselves. That is part of their path. You have a path to follow, too. Or maybe you don't. Find it and stay on it until you arrive. Don't let this book or anything else guide you. A guide knows where he or she is going. But how can another person truly know where I am going if I am the only one who can look inside myself and figure this out?

CHAPTER 5
HEALTH & FITNESS

"She ate healthy and worked out, but still died from a terminal disease at a young age . . ." Torrey Lee

I am not exactly sure why this chapter on health and fitness is in this book. I have lost hope on this issue. At about 24 years of age, I became more conscious of my health. I was already running three to five times a week, at least nine miles each run. I remember running with guys who had trained for the U.S. Olympics. They asked me why I would not train and compete, given that I was running at a semi-professional level. All I could tell them was that I loved going out to run so I could listen to my music, think about my love affairs, look at the people who were watching me, and act in all the other unrestrictive ways that you can't when you are training to compete. I was convinced to compete for a spot on the college team. I met with the coach for the mandatory physical that all athletes undergo, and was told my blood pressure was a little high for my age. I immediately stopped eating pork and started taking vitamins and supplements. That was the beginning of my living a healthy life. Whole Foods, the organic/natural food store, had not yet arrived in Tennessee, USA. There was a small local organic/natural food store, but organic food was expensive and not yet popular in this region of the country. Most of the people in the store were older, and upper-class, so to speak. The people I knew thought organic food was nasty and would say things like, "Give me the food with chemicals in it." You are laughing right now, but this actually happened. Some of the women I dated would crack jokes about me as well. All this was before eating healthy became a trend in America. Even when it comes to health, people follow trends as opposed to the facts of their own bodies.

On any given day, you can see young men and women who are not training for any competitive sport or body competition working out at a gym. The gym craze has doubled, with people waking up extra early or coming in very late to work out. At two times in my life, I built up muscle mass and worked out profusely. One of those times I was taking supplements, and the other I was eating everything I wanted in large portions. It made me feel good to stare at my arms and see who was staring at me. At the time, I believed that I could have more love affairs as a result of my physicality and outward strength. This idea had me convinced that somehow those things were a representation of my inner strength. All of this, of course, was inaccurate for me.

Camera phones have made it extremely easy for people to worship their bodies and the bodies of others. Go to any popular social media site and you will see many pictures of women and men posing in various ways. Some of these people base all of their decisions, emotions, and thoughts on the feeling of not measuring up physically.

I won't say it's what's on the inside that counts, because most people already have some idea of this. But, in short, here's what I will say about eating healthy and working out: Feeling good and being good, as opposed to looking good, are two different concepts. Why should you stress yourself on outward looks for someone who probably does not like the inner you? Why would you want this person to lust after you, hang out with you, or praise you? You can eat healthily, exercise, and take supplements, but if you are not on a path to discovering yourself, loving yourself in the process, and loving what you find, then what the hell are you trying to stay alive for?

Bonus: That little voice inside of you is telling you what you should be . . .

It may be telling you that having an ass like Kim Kardashian or a body like The Rock won't fulfil you. Maybe you should listen to that voice, or not. Of course, do what the hell you want with your body!

CHAPTER 6
POOR & RICH

"Since neither the terms rich or poor have a defined amount, how do I know if I am truly one or the other???"
Torrey Lee

L et's all be rich. Let's all have as much money as we can stand. In the United States, money is in your face from the time you are born until the time you die, when we open our mail, pass billboards, watch television, and even worship. For a lot of people, money is the root of everything they do, think, and represent about themselves. Money enables people to pursue so many great causes, and if it didn't, it would be easy for us to consider it to be evil on the basis of our individual moralities. Money saves people's lives, feeds people, and brings family and friends together. At the same time, we can use money to buy drugs, have sex of any kind, hire an assassin, ruin someone's social image, become the president of the United States or any country, avoid paying the price for a crime committed, and many other immoral things.

Consider a slogan like, "Money can't buy you love," which I disagree with. Let's say I am in love with someone, and because of my money, they love me more than someone else who claims to love me for another reason. In that case, I will take the former. Does that sound terrible? Maybe, but that's just your opinion. I think the main point is that you have to love yourself. I don't think we can prove or know whether people really love us or identify exactly what they love us for. I think the things that people do and say help us believe we are loved. Those things can often be traced back to money. Are you doubting me?

Let's take a look. You are in a romantic relationship, and because of money, you can fly your lover to some of the most beautiful places in the world. The times you spend together at those places are truly magical, because of the afforded extras your money can buy. Your lover feels secure because your money suggests to them that, in any situation, they can trust you have the means to accommodate them. Your lover makes you feel like they are happy. Now, is love really present and is it the basis for that relationship? Maybe or maybe not. But you know how you feel, and you know how that person makes you feel. The last ingredient is their feelings. If your lover's feelings (at least what they tell you they feel) and actions align, then what would be different in the case of a relationship that was not built on money? The issue is not only theoretical but also moral, particularly if it conflicts with your beliefs.

This argument supports those individuals who claim that money, not the pursuit of money, but money in and of itself, is the essence of their happiness. I have two responses to people in those situations: (1) Don't run out of money or ways to acquire money. (2) As for relationships, just hope that your lover does not either begin to love someone else who has more money, or come to love someone for something other than money.

Some people say that the poor are the scum of the Earth. I disagree. We have to take care of the poor, right? We get up for work and make sacrifices that involve our family, friends, morals, comforts, and bodies. Some people say those bastards are just living at our expense. (Funny, I feel as though someone else has inhabited my body as I write this. If this was true, would I be conscious of this?)

This is the concept of dog versus master. When you see a person walking a dog, you may wonder, who is walking who? Who is the master? The dog sleeps and eats at his or her master's expense. You might say that the dog cannot do whatever it wants to do, but neither can humans. In theory, both can, but what we really mean is do whatever each wants without having to face any consequences that we deem undesirable. The poorer a person is, the less they seem to have to worry about. Yes, they have to worry about food, shelter, love, security, and perhaps environmental issues. I can see where not having these things, or routinely not having access to them, would prevent the poor from worrying about them as often, or, after a period of time, not at all. Those worries apply to rich people as well. The poor generally have fewer responsibilities than the rich, that is, in terms of quantity. Think of shelters, charities, and low-income-based housing tenements. Hang out with poor people and you will find that they can still receive happiness, love, sex, purpose in life, friends, family, and faith/religion. The poor can lose the things they have as well.

What I think really gets everyone mad is that the poor make us question why we really work hard and sacrifice. You may see a really beautiful woman with a guy who appears to be poor, or a person you know to be poor who is always surrounded by happy friends and family, or a poor guy who is always smiling. Some poor people are convinced that they will not be happy or have a better life until they become what they believe their idea of rich is. Some people are loaded with money and are happy. Some are miserable.

It is easy to tell people to recognize the important things in life. If, however, the pursuit of money is the point of life to someone, then so be it. I have had things, but I have not experienced real financial wealth. Which for me means that your money works for you and there is enough to last for the rest of your life, kid's lives, and grandkids lives. Somehow, I managed to get some of the things that the rich have like owning multiple houses, luxury cars, owning businesses, placing my daughters in very expensive private schools, and wearing tailor-made clothing. But I also lost some of those things and still had something more valuable: My life! I enjoyed waking up to read, exercise, laugh with companions and strangers, eat healthily, make love, drink, dream, plan, fail, cry, hurt, explore, travel, believe, hope, volunteer, pursue new hobbies, fantasize, have romance, learn, and do many more things. So, what's the difference? I am not quite sure there is a real difference between being rich or poor. Both can lose what they have, and both can acquire more or not acquire more.

Leo Tolstoy, one of the greatest writers of all time, rejected his inherited and earned wealth. He even gave up the copyright to his earlier works, due to what he claimed to be a spiritual awakening. Towards the end of his career, in 1901, Tolstoy was selected to receive the first Nobel Prize in Literature, but he turned down the honour in October of the same year, worried that the prize money would bring unwanted complications to his life.

I bet you think I am going to bring up that inner voice. Nope. Redundancy is for kids and idiots.

CHAPTER 7
FEAR & COURAGE

"I am afraid to die because I have never met someone who has been dead mentally and physically for some years, who then came back to life and could clearly explain what death is like." Torrey Lee

I t has taken me weeks to write this chapter. Why? We could say I was afraid, or we could say that I had the courage to take my time. So, what is fear? What is courage? And what is the difference between the two? How do you know when you experience fear or courage? And what do they feel like? As you have been reading, you may have gotten the idea that I have used fear indirectly as an excuse or as an explanation as to why people don't look inside themselves. Is that really an accurate assessment?

Fear keeps people from doing things, but so does courage. Fear makes people unhappy, but so does courage. Some people love to live in fear and some people love to live courageously. There has to be something that separates these two traits. (I refuse to research the topic because that would be a breach of my contract with the Divine, who is writing this book through me!) By acknowledging both fear and courage, the difference is ever so clear: There isn't any difference at all; not a single one. The two don't even exist. The two words are just mere variations of our feelings about why we do things and why we don't. In other words, the words good and bad and fear and courage are the same thing. This is not merely a case of subjective interpretation. Then, again, maybe it is.

A teenager once shared a story with me when we were both 16 years old. He and a friend had been charged with killing another teen in a game of craps. I asked the usual questions that any person might have asked: Why did you do it? (I only asked him why because he volunteered that he did it without my even having asked. That's freaking crazy, but this is accurate.) His answer was that the victim "was making fun of us while winning our money." I asked whether he had nightmares about the situation. His reply was, "No, I sleep fine." He shot and killed the other 14-year-old male at point-blank range.

Now, let's look at this situation from a fear standpoint. One could argue that he was afraid of being ridiculed and losing at the same time. His fear prompted him to kill. Or, we could say that he had the courage to honour the code of the streets and not let anyone berate him or, to use the street terminology, to punk him. So, which is it? They both could have produced the same result, just originating from different vantage points. The idea of fear and courage both come from the inner soul. The soul is not subjective. It is concrete, objective, and anything else that best describes something of certainty!

The soul isn't something that is altered with the wind. It's a mix of pre-set Divine components, metaphysical ingredients, environmental influences, spirits, and beliefs. Some of those elements may be abstract or concrete but mixed together, they comprise the soul in and of itself. Does that mean that the teen's soul was evil? I would say no. His case is extreme, but millions if not billions of people do the same thing, or they allow the same thing to happen to them every day. It is the woman who gets married when really her soul is suited to being a missionary and not a housewife. It is the man who deep down knows he is gay but marries a woman and has children. I knew a woman who was married to a guy who my friends thought was gay from the start. They divorced because he was having a relationship with another man. Was he confused? Afraid? Or, did he have the courage to try to be a heterosexual male?

Those scenarios are all the same. They just didn't kill another person. Possibly, they just killed themselves, so to speak. Who was that young teen really? A killer? I would say possibly not. Our actions don't change our soul. They either make it highly visible or invisible to ourselves, and others, in the world. He was a blind teen who had become a monster as a result of God knows what. Had someone pushed him to seek out his soul, then maybe that situation would have been different. It's not necessarily anyone else's fault either, but the feelings of fear or courage kept him blind to his soul. The next time you have what you perceive as feelings of fear or courage, ask yourself whether you're doing something that leads you to your soul or away from it. Again, I would stay away from books, people, or anything that claims to illustrate how to listen to, discover, and understand your soul. I think life is about experiencing and figuring that out on your own. If you really knew how much your soul was worth, you would use every resource available within you to understand it, accept it, and follow it. You might want to think twice before you sell your soul. (If one can really do that anyway!) I had to throw that lousy ass statement in there. The idiotic and dumb statements we accept! Those of you wondering how I had that conversation with the teen killer, let's just say I took a week-long vacation at an all-inclusive resort paid for by the government. The food was horrible, and the resort had a lot of damn rules, extra security, and limited amenities.

Bonus: If you still don't understand any of what I just wrote, consider this . . .

The issue isn't just about defining fear or courage, and I don't think it ever will be about conquering one challenge or rising to another. It will always be about what these challenges mean to an individual and how they cause a person to feel, live, die, do, or not do. Perhaps I should have said that at the start of this chapter instead of wasting your time with all the rest of these words. But maybe I didn't have the courage!

CHAPTER 8
CONCLUSION

"I think the most powerful people in the world chose not to read this book, or they bought it and have simply stopped reading it by now." Torrey Lee

Some say that we all have a choice. I have always had a problem with the thought of having the choice to choose to be something. As a young man, I was troubled because I believed that our choices in this life are limited. Did you choose to be born, choose your parents, gender, physical features, or your race? When you really think about it a lot of things are chosen for us. It is easy for a person to say I chose to be a doctor. Did they really? Sure, anyone can become a doctor. But what actually makes one a doctor? The license? The degree? What about a woman who has spent a great deal of her life doing one thing, and suddenly changes to something else? She may have been a grant writer and did really well at it. Yet she was not able to erase the burning desire to treat people through the practice of medicine. My younger daughter's school was full of people who are worth millions and billions of dollars, and the first question everybody asks is, "What do you do?" I'm not sure whether they ask this to size you up as a person, start a pissing contest, or simply to start a conversation. I once met a gentleman whose son went to the school. At a parent mixer, he shared his career story with me. He said he was an engineer and was doing quite well at it. Then midway through his forties, he quit his job and went to medical school and became a gastroenterologist. As you read this, you probably can think of someone who has had a similar experience. This may sound radical, but I don't give a rat's ass. We don't have a choice about what our souls are. We didn't make our soul, and there isn't a philosophical or scientific piece of writing in this world that can convince me that we can change it.

There's peace and happiness in acknowledging what our souls were pre-set to do. Hence, the idea that dogs are happy all the time. Have you ever seen a dog, even with human manipulation, be anything else but a dog? The choice we have to make is one of misery or happiness. Shit, sometimes—I must admit— I feel powerless at both of those options! People can do things outside of what their soul was destined for and can experience great feelings of happiness.

Feelings of happiness and fulfilment, again, are totally different concepts. We can experience the supernatural elements in life when we are living in line with our soul. We can be aware of many things around us that, with no action or interaction from us, give confirmation to and aid our existence.

Let's say, for example, that your soul was pre-set for you to be able to sing. Naturally, you are able to do things with your voice that a person who practices for years can never do. That's what makes our souls so special. Our souls have supernatural power. Science cannot explain or produce formulas for our souls, either. At least not yet, anyway.

The hard but rewarding part is this journey to our soul. That's what this whole book has been about. This book actually helped me confirm the discovery of my soul. I spent years trying to find it, running from it, and not accepting it. I was looking everywhere and had no clue it was right here with me. It is not hidden; it's just buried. For me at least, the issue is that I really didn't want to find it, and I didn't want to do the work required to dig it up. For your soul to come to fruition you may have to go around the world, out of this world, and into this world. You might have to go through hell and be lost for some time in this world. Taking this journey is the most valuable thing a person can do. You should not leave your soul buried. Corporations dig every day for diamonds, jewels, and all kinds of raw materials. Whether or not you believe me, your soul is worth more than diamonds or anything else this world's physical properties can offer. It contains all of your jewels, your unique identification, your purpose, your passion, and your secrets. It's your treasure chest. Your soul is your blueprint. Once I discovered and accepted mine, I came into my own. I became alive in this life physically, mentally, and spiritually. I had been living, but I was not yet soulfully alive. This is the crowning achievement of existence. It is being totally aware consciously and subconsciously at the same time. Your soul is everything that represents your being. The best way to describe it can be compared to this: It's like being a ball of fire, consuming, but not being consumed. My whole being is illuminated.

In the title, I told you to throw this book away. Here is why. This book is nothing more than a glimpse into my world. It is not a map, a guide, or advice. Not only should you throw away this book, but you should also throw away all self-help, religious, and philosophical books, unless your soul has told you that you need one as a piece to your life's puzzle. No one can help you discover your soul. That work is actually what makes the journey so special. People can share their stories and ideals with you, as I have done, but don't try and use their experiences and rules for your life.

If you are lost right now, you can enjoy and embrace being in this state. Or complain, be depressed, sad, or angry. Do what you shall, but under no circumstances should you allow someone else to tell you how to come into your own. Now, throw this damn book in the trash. If you don't, you risk referring to it, rather than listening to yourself.

ABOUT THE AUTHOR

Torrey Lee was born in Nashville, Tennessee, and has two daughters. As a young man, he tried to study what would yield a great job or acquire business opportunities, and later ran several small businesses. Eventually, Torrey found peace studying Philosophy at the Middle TN State University. He believes that being a small business owner gave him the ability to throw himself completely into his studies, reading many books at once.

At the end of 2017, he started traveling the world, bringing validation to theories produced while studying in and out of college. Torrey has lived on three continents outside of North America, and currently resides in South East Asia.

This is not Torrey's first book. In his youth, he wrote a book about his life. However, he decided not to publish it. The reason? "Not everything should be for sale, and some artwork is just for the artist."

Email: torrey@iffybooks.com